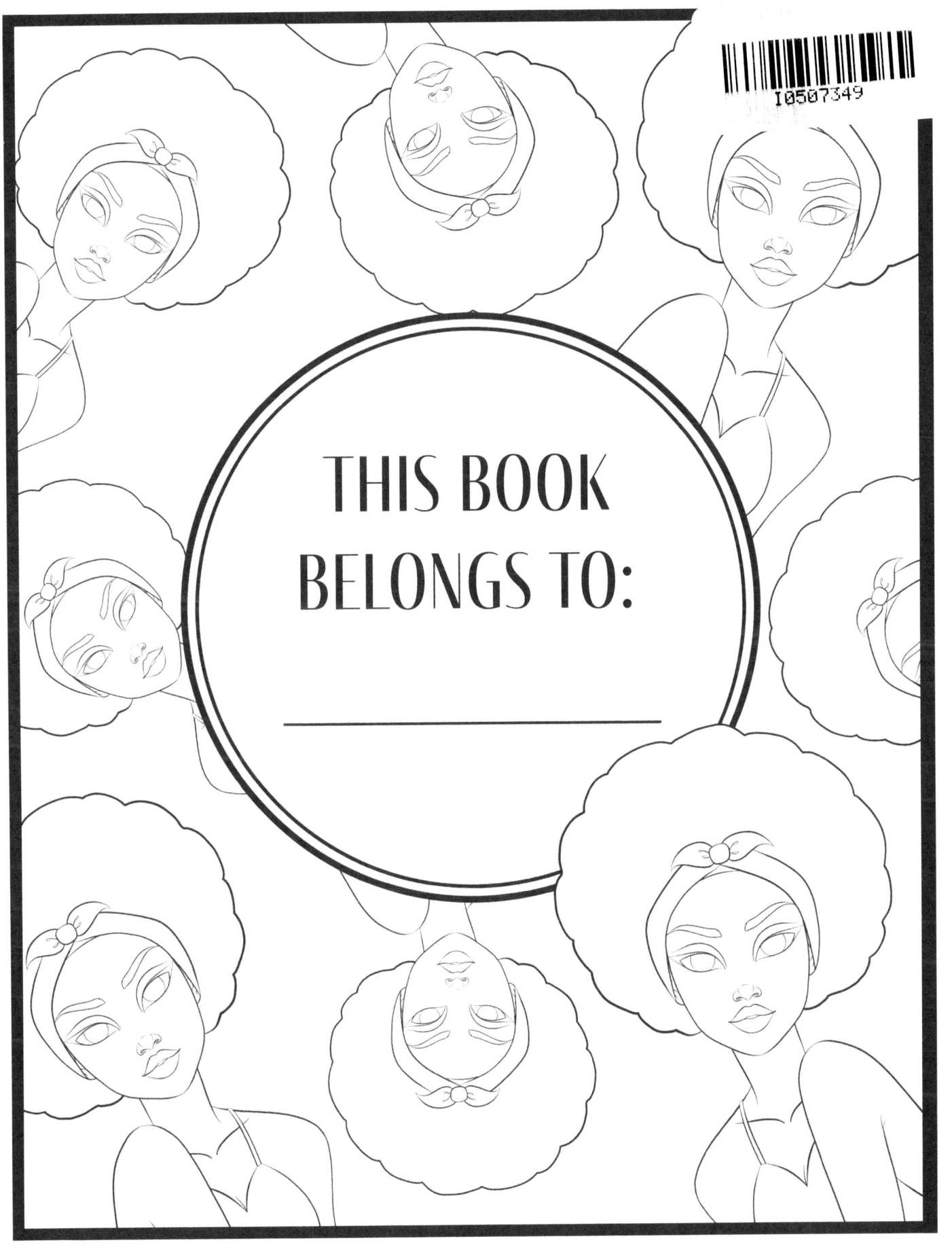

COPYRIGHT 2021 BY BROOKE RANKINS/BROOKESCANVAS

ALL RIGHTS RESERVED. NO PART OF THIS BOOK MAY BE REPRODUCED OR USED IN ANY MANNER WITHOUT WRITTEN PERMISSION OF THE COPYRIGHT OWNER.

DESIGNED AND ILLUSTRATED BY BROOKE RANKINS
ISBN: 9798742800965 (PAPERBACK)
PUBLISHED BY BROOKE RANKINS
WWW.BROOKESCANVAS.COM

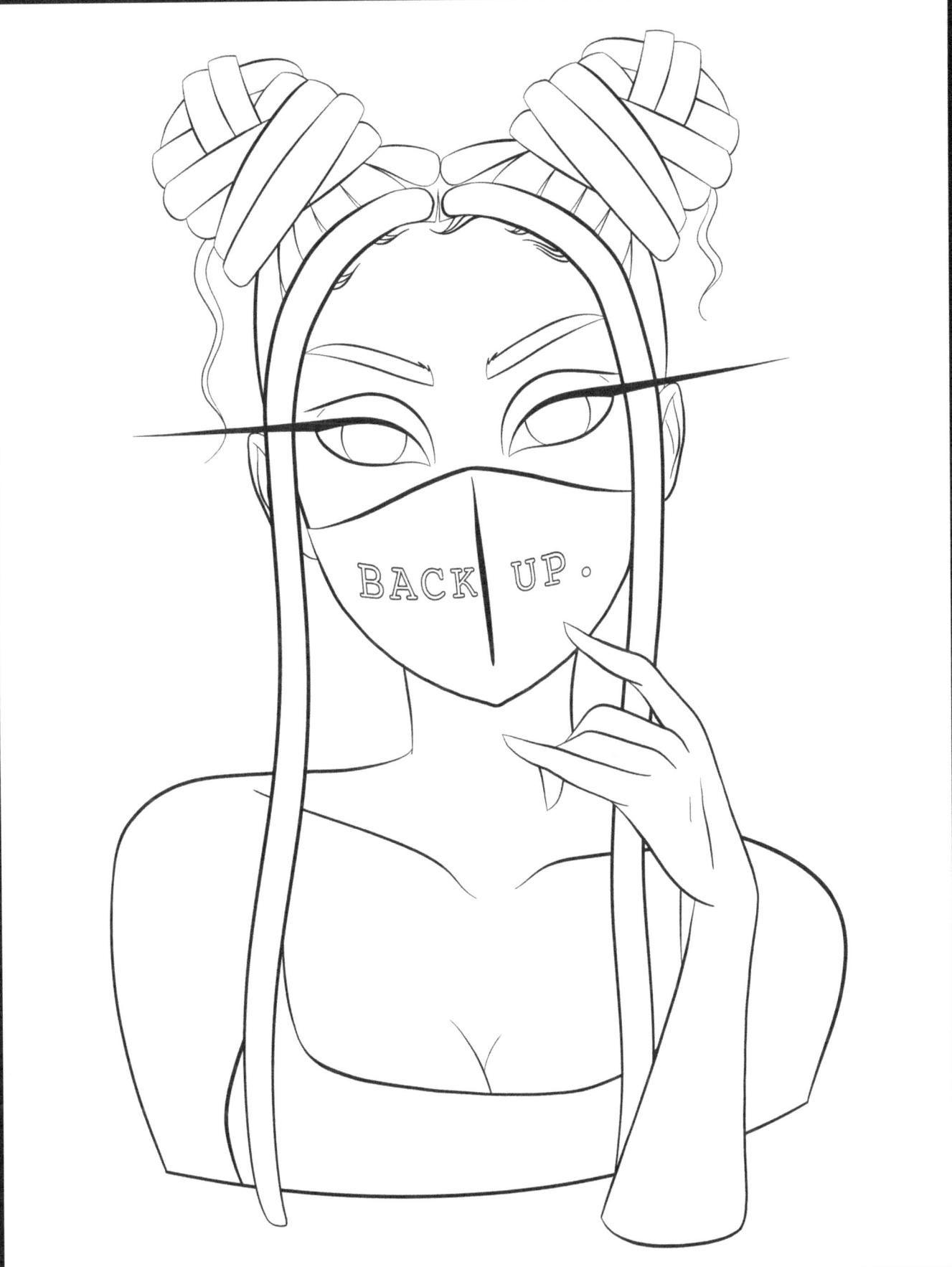

I AM UNIQUE.

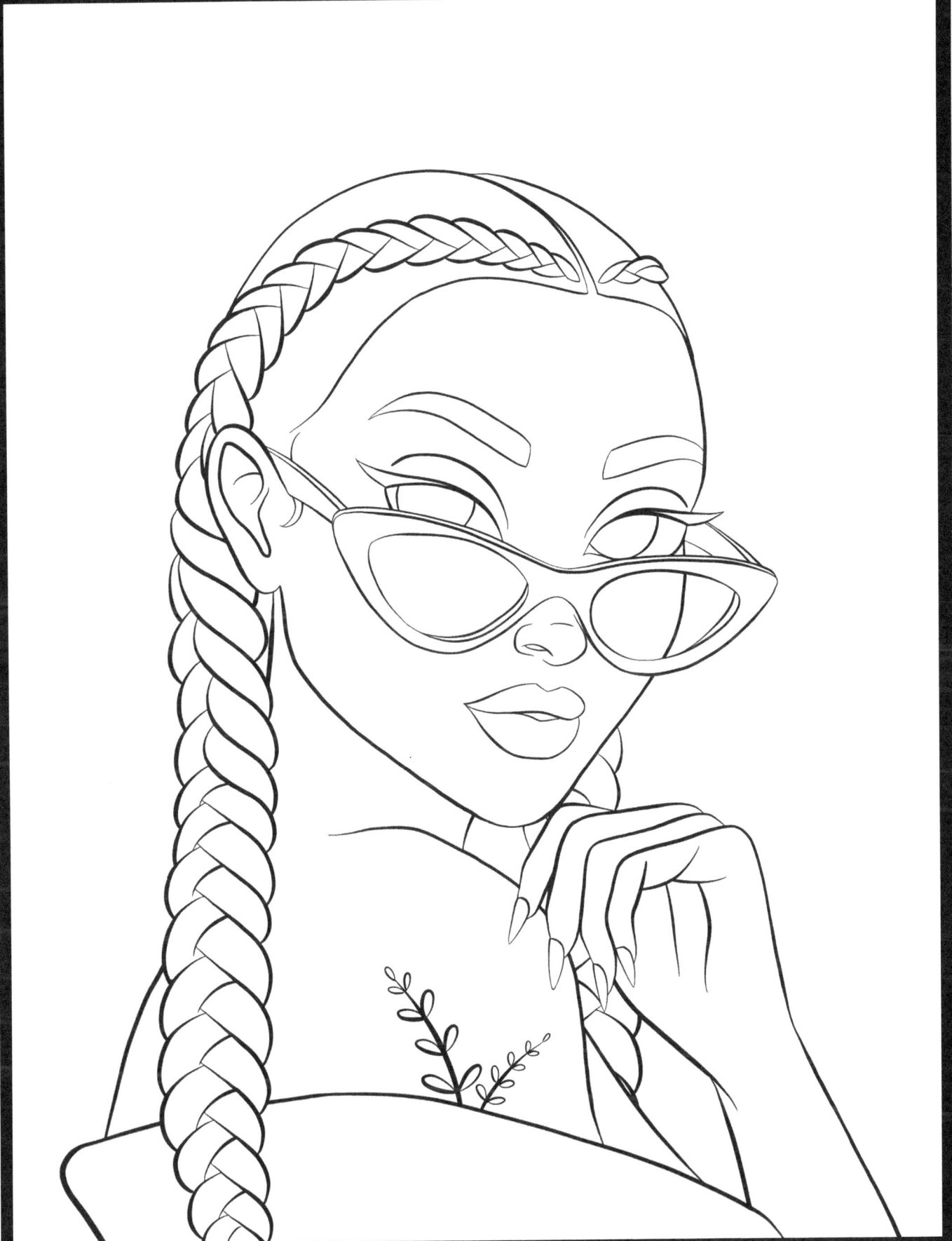

I AM GLORIOUS.

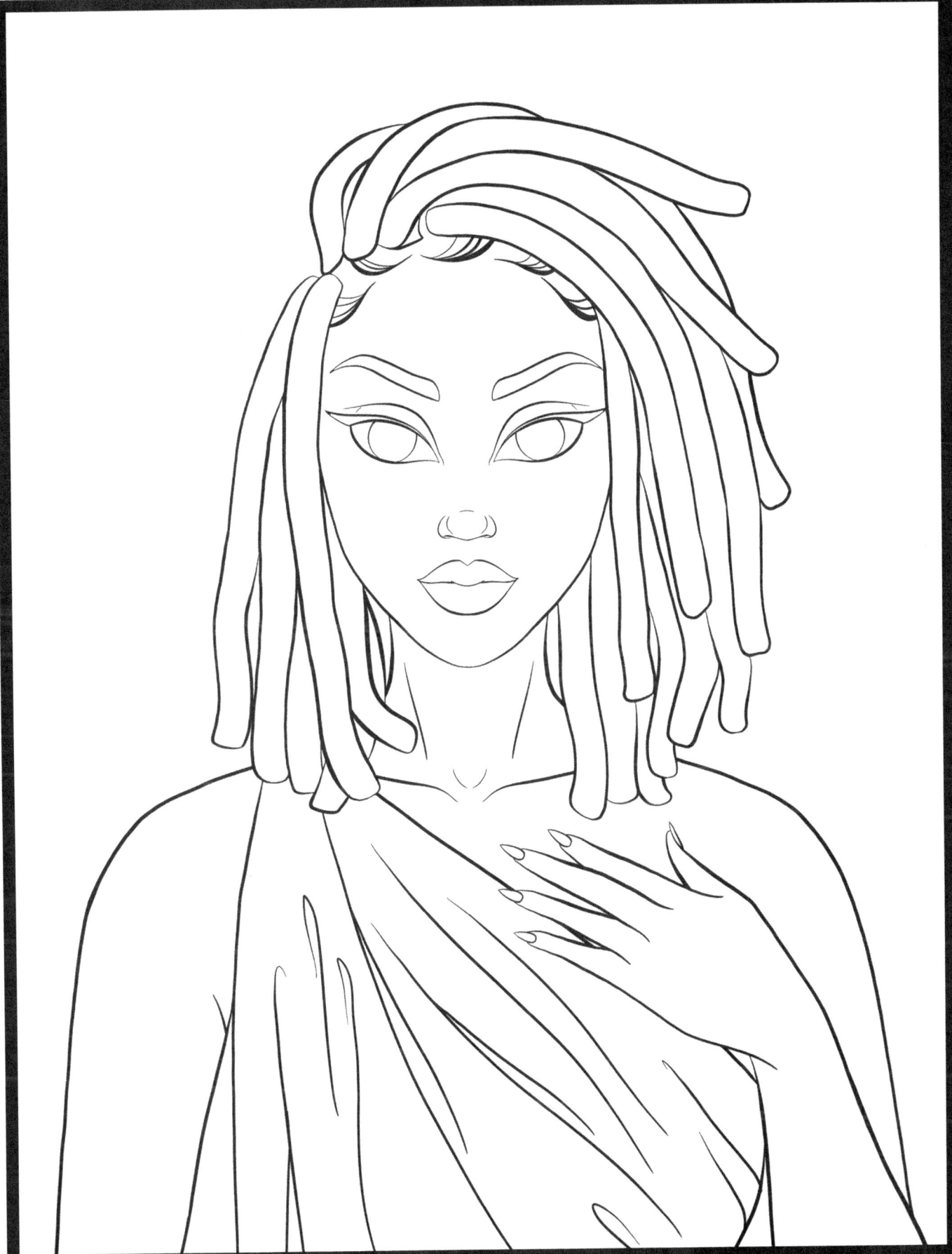

I AM FIERCE.

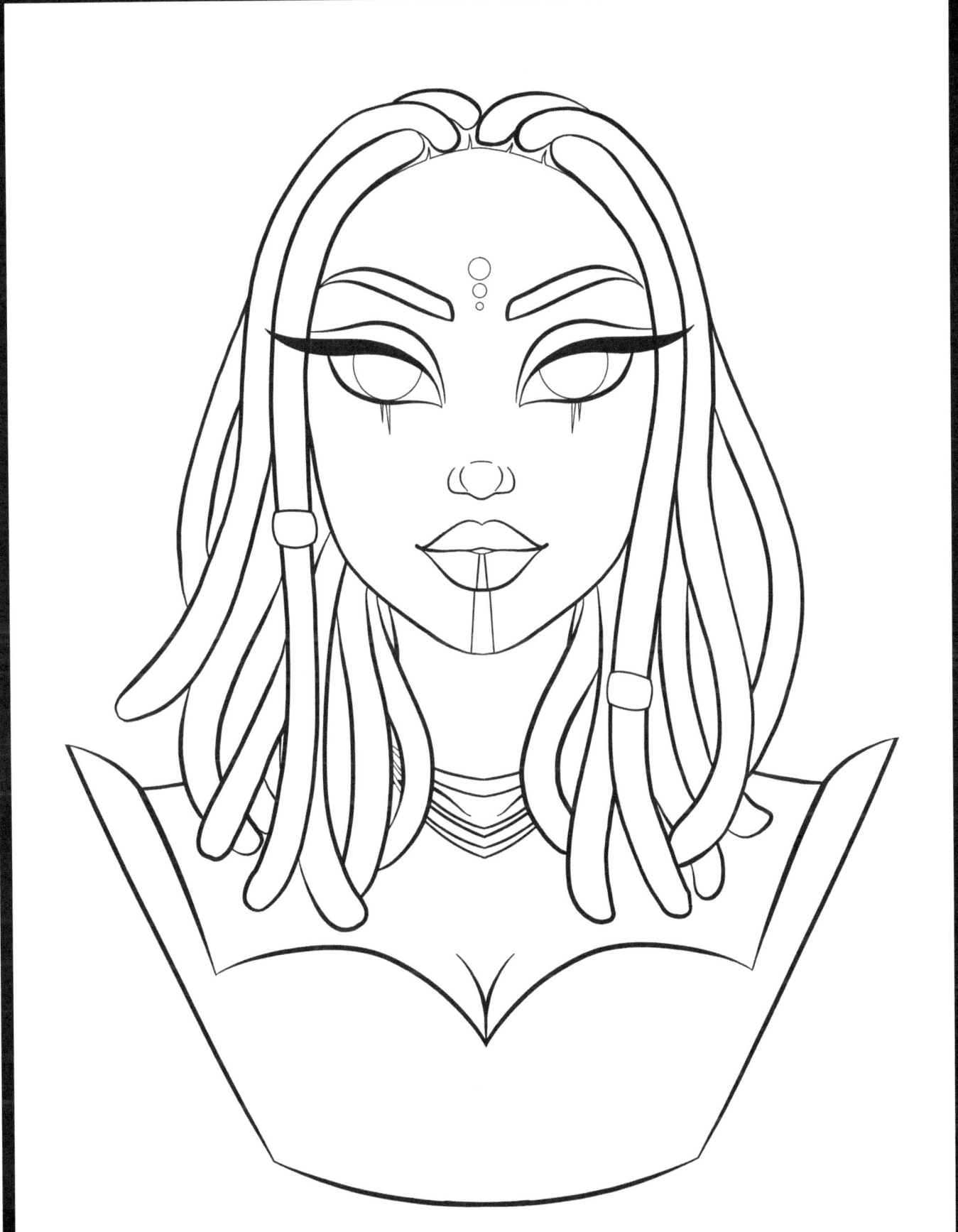

I AM A DREAMER.

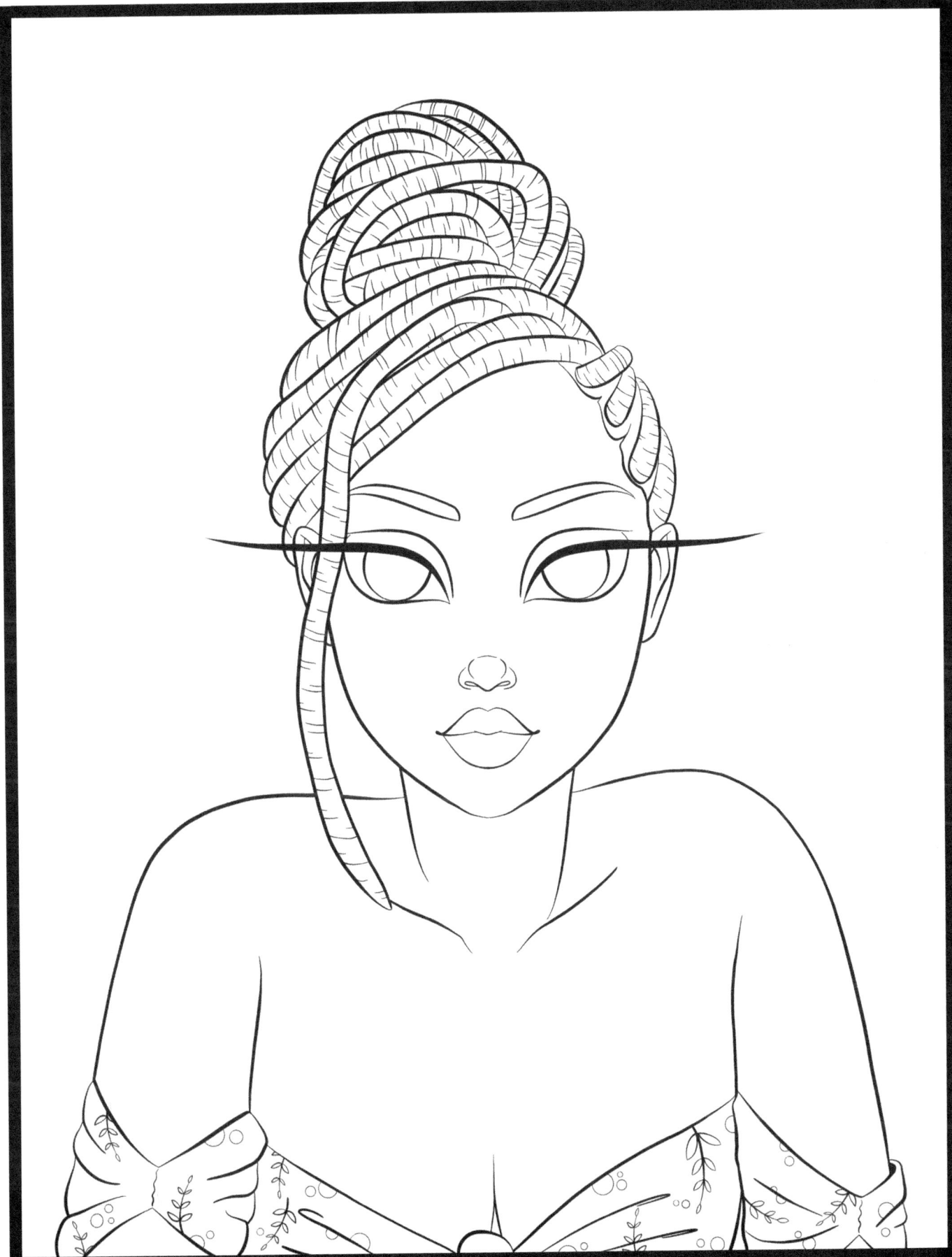

I AM EVERYTHING.

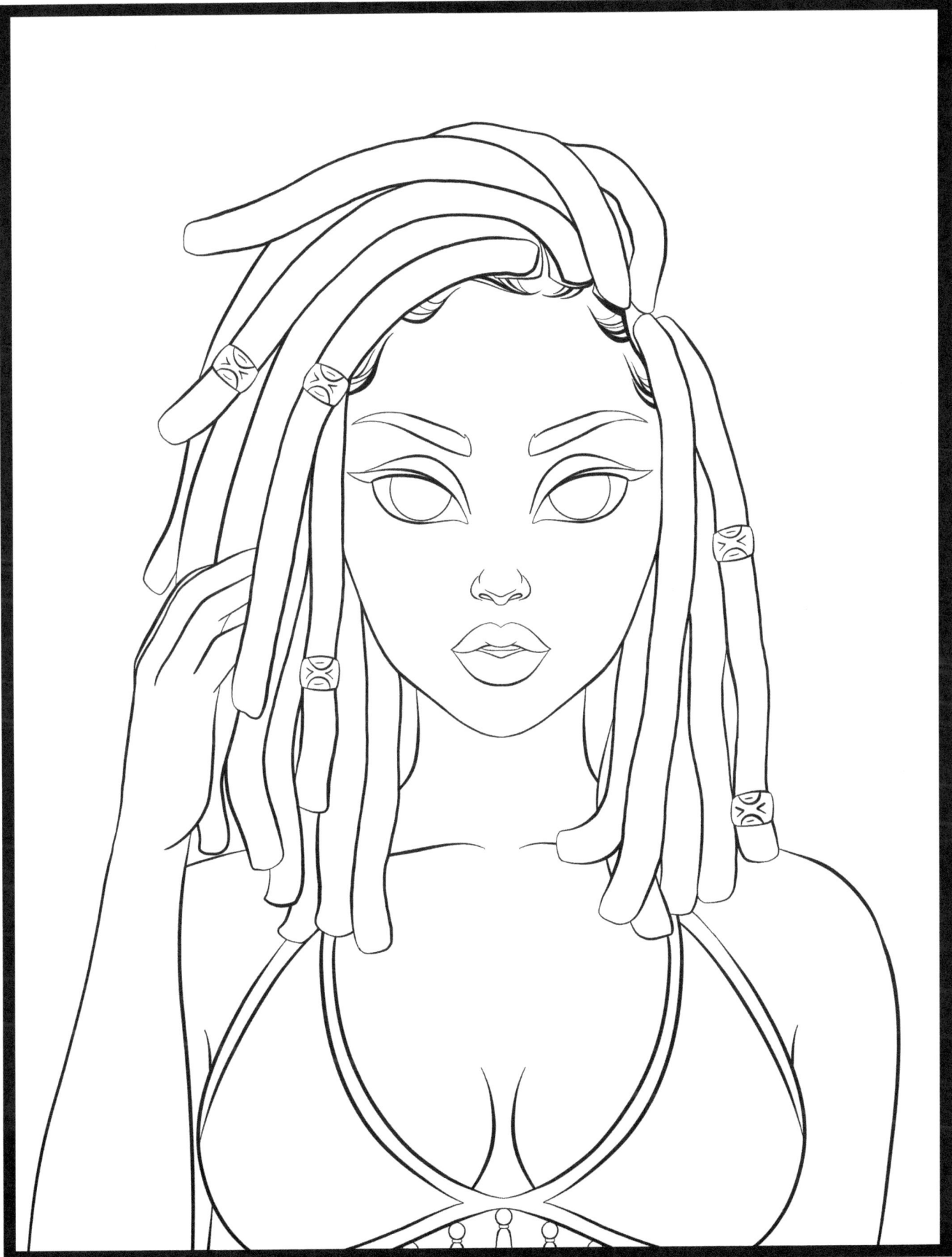

I AM UNAPOLOGETICALLY ME.

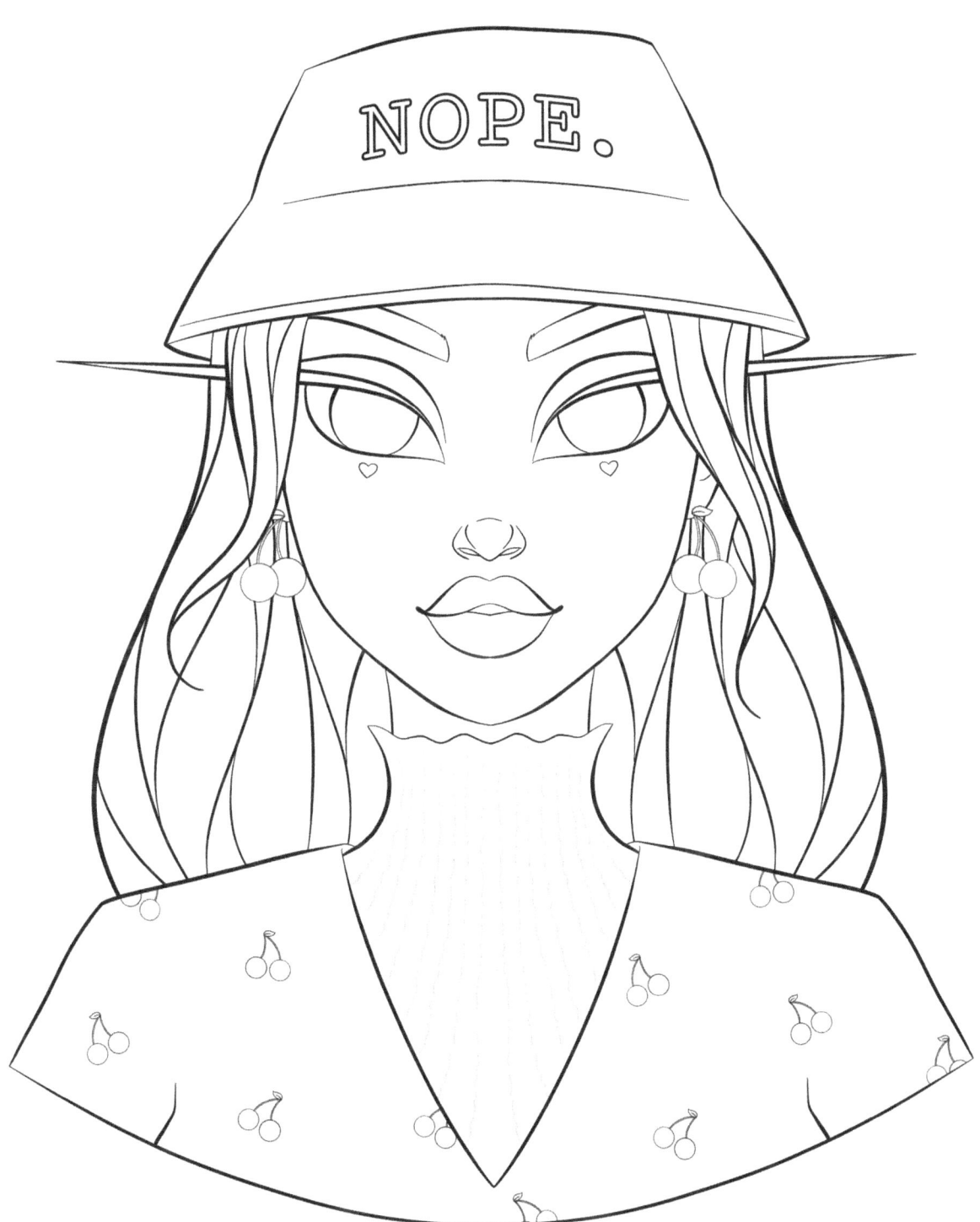

I AM A BOSS.

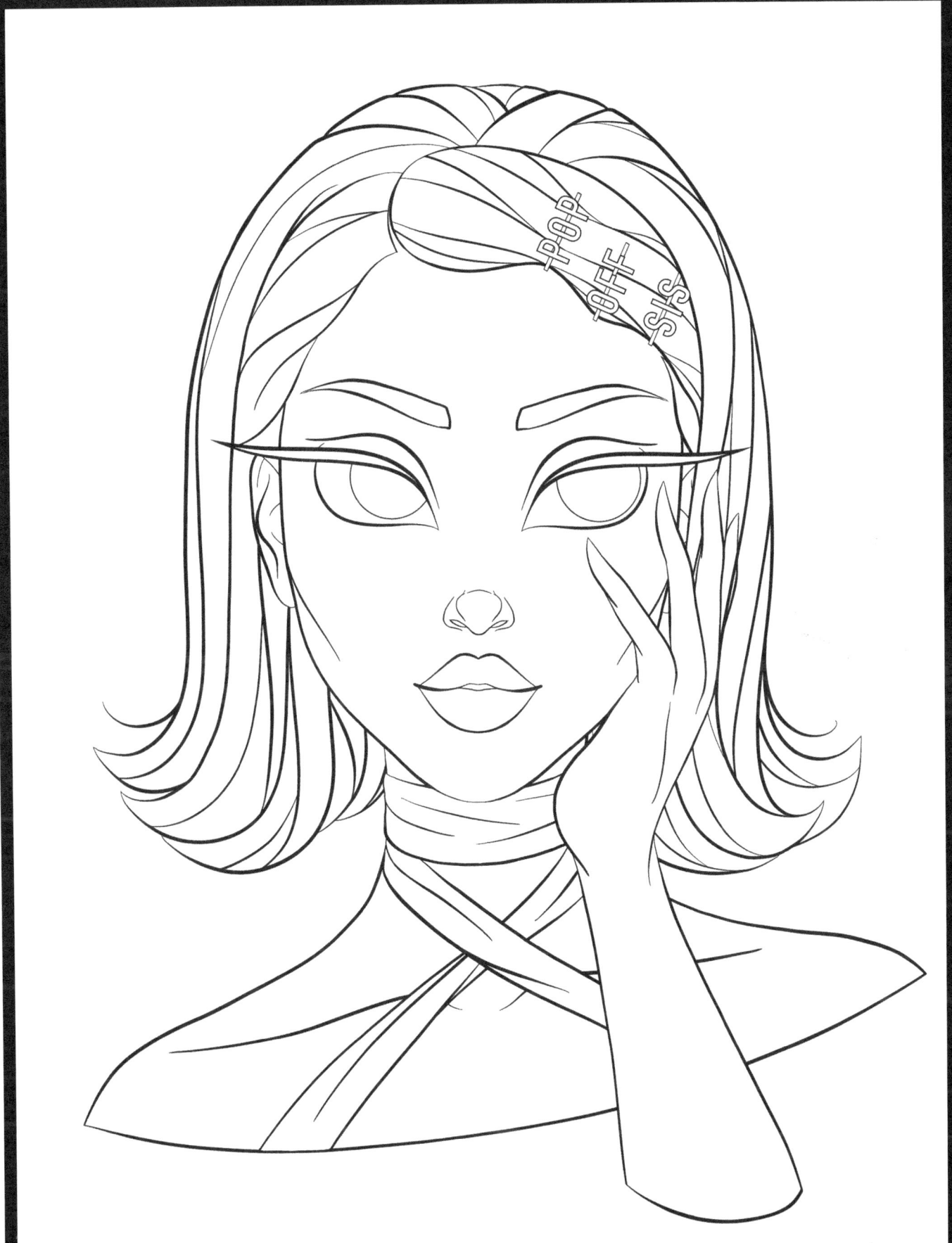

MY LIFE IS LIMITLESS.

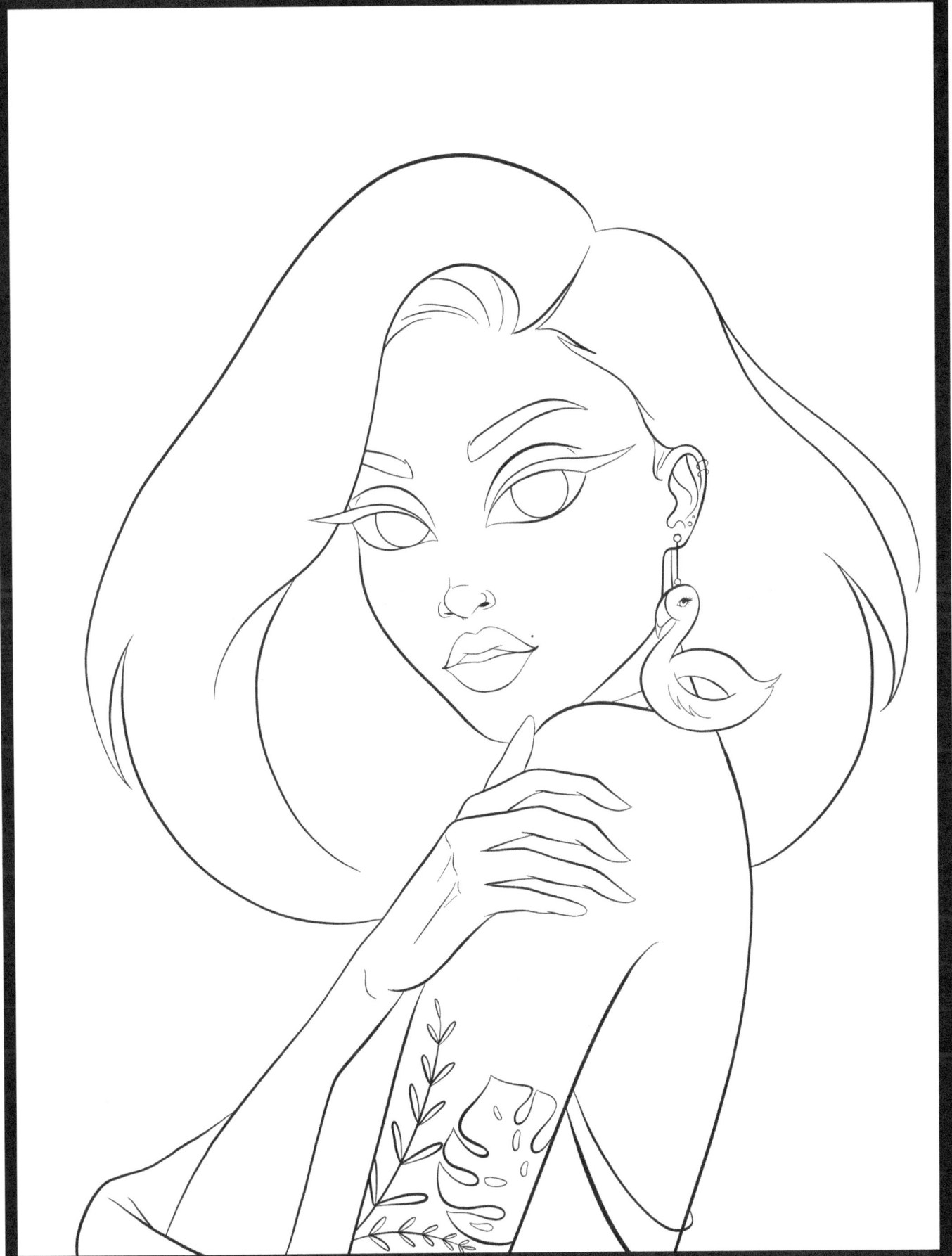

I AM POWERFUL.

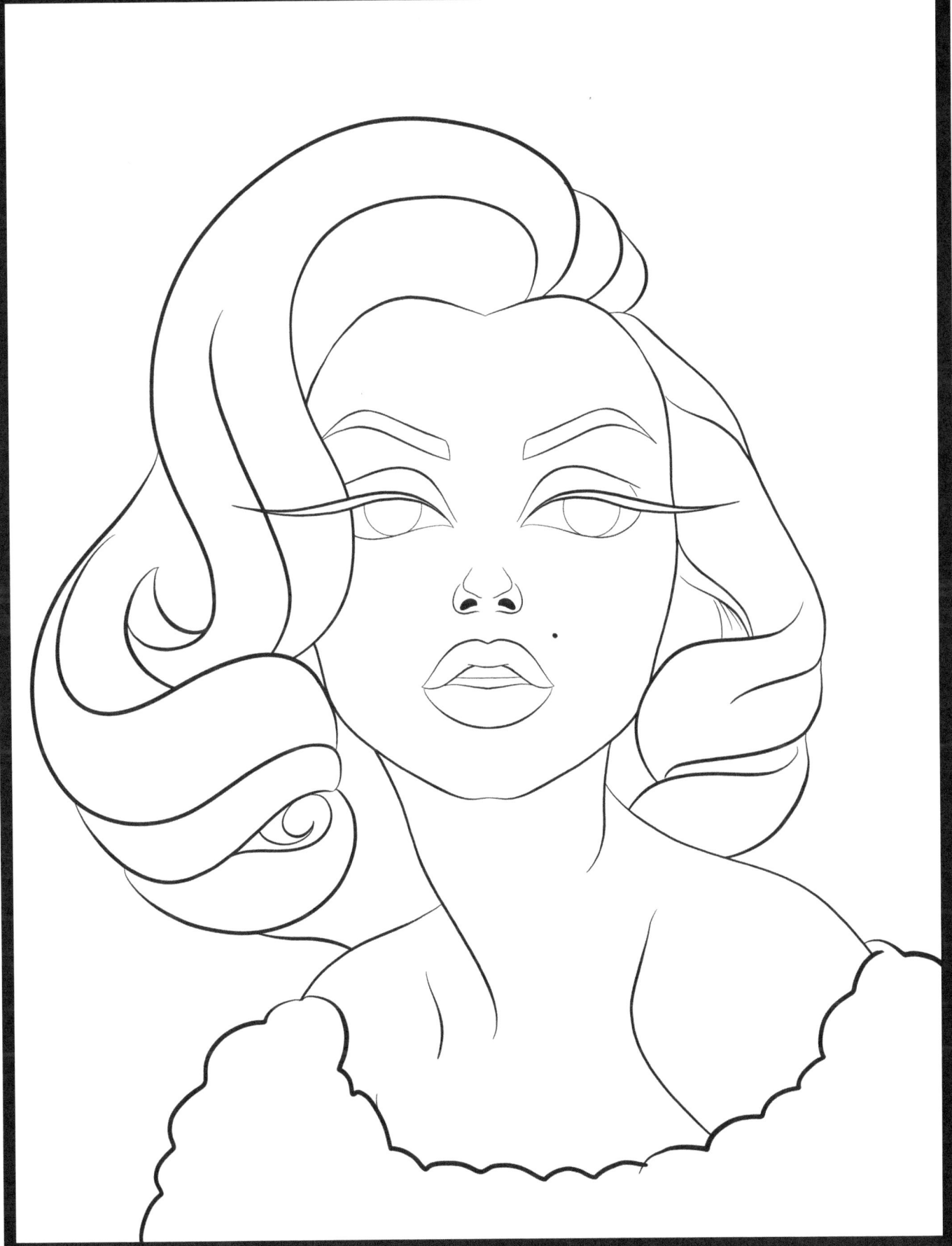

MY ENERGY IS RADIANT.

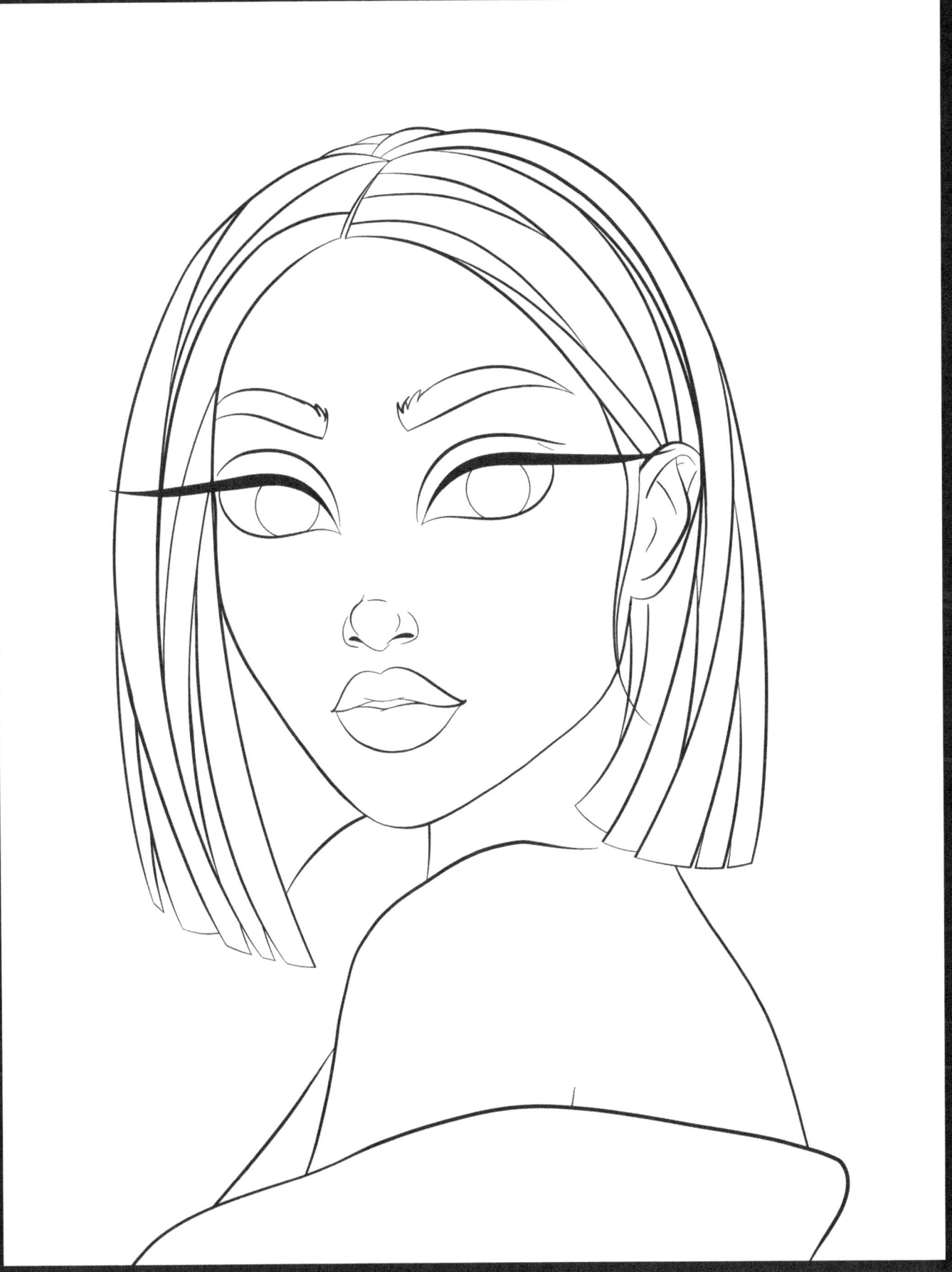

I AM UNSTOPPABLE.

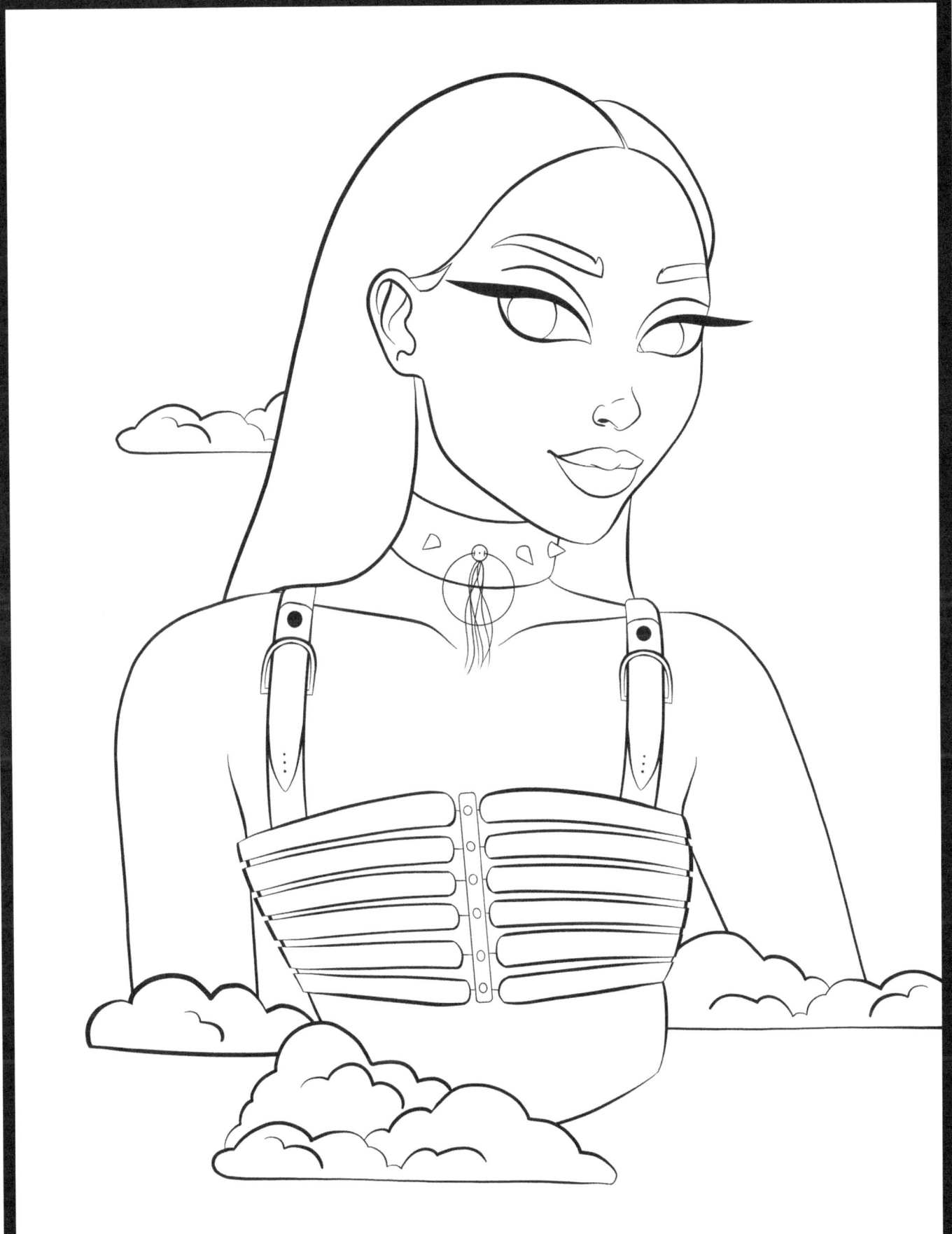

I AM EMPOWERED.

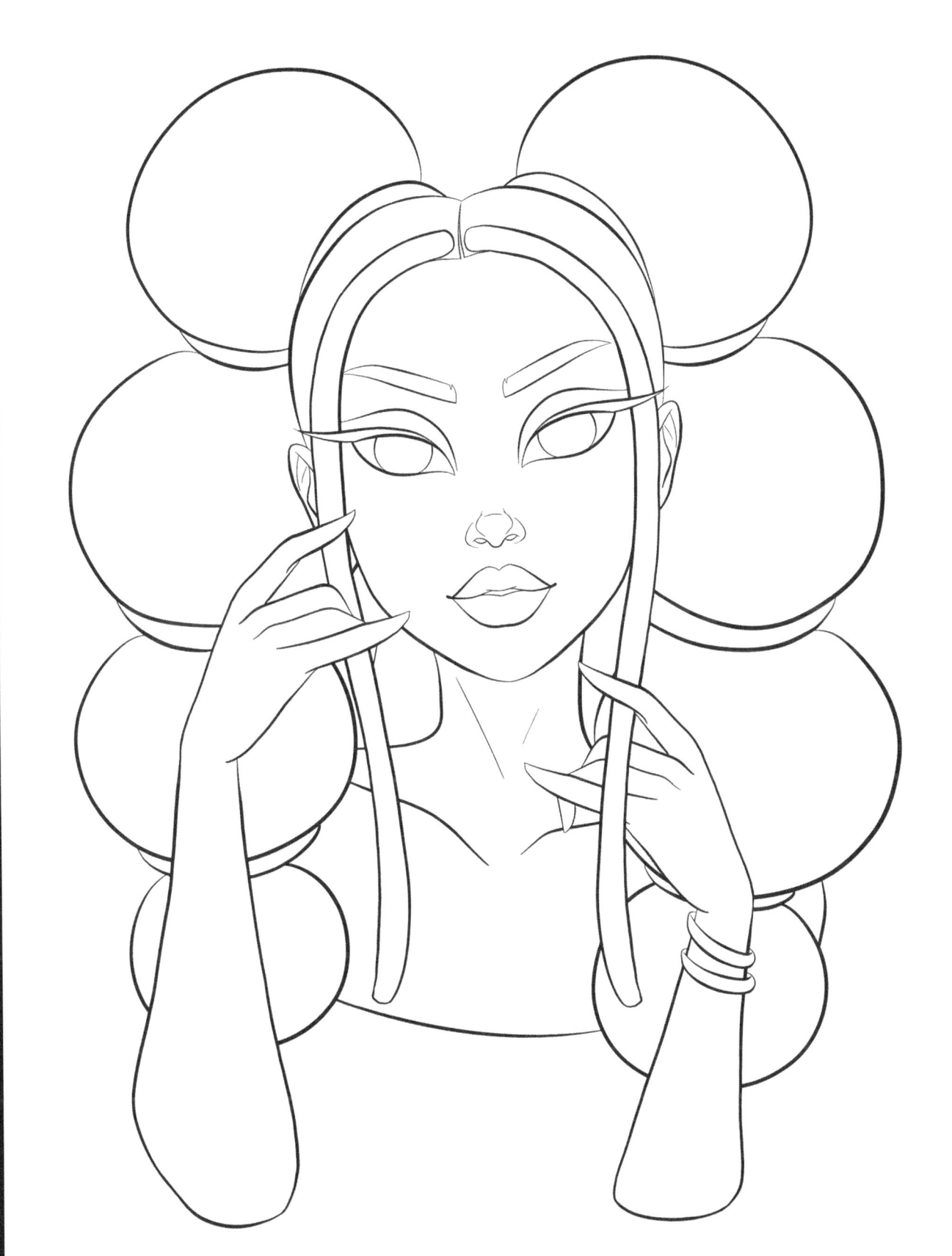

I AM BEAUTIFUL.

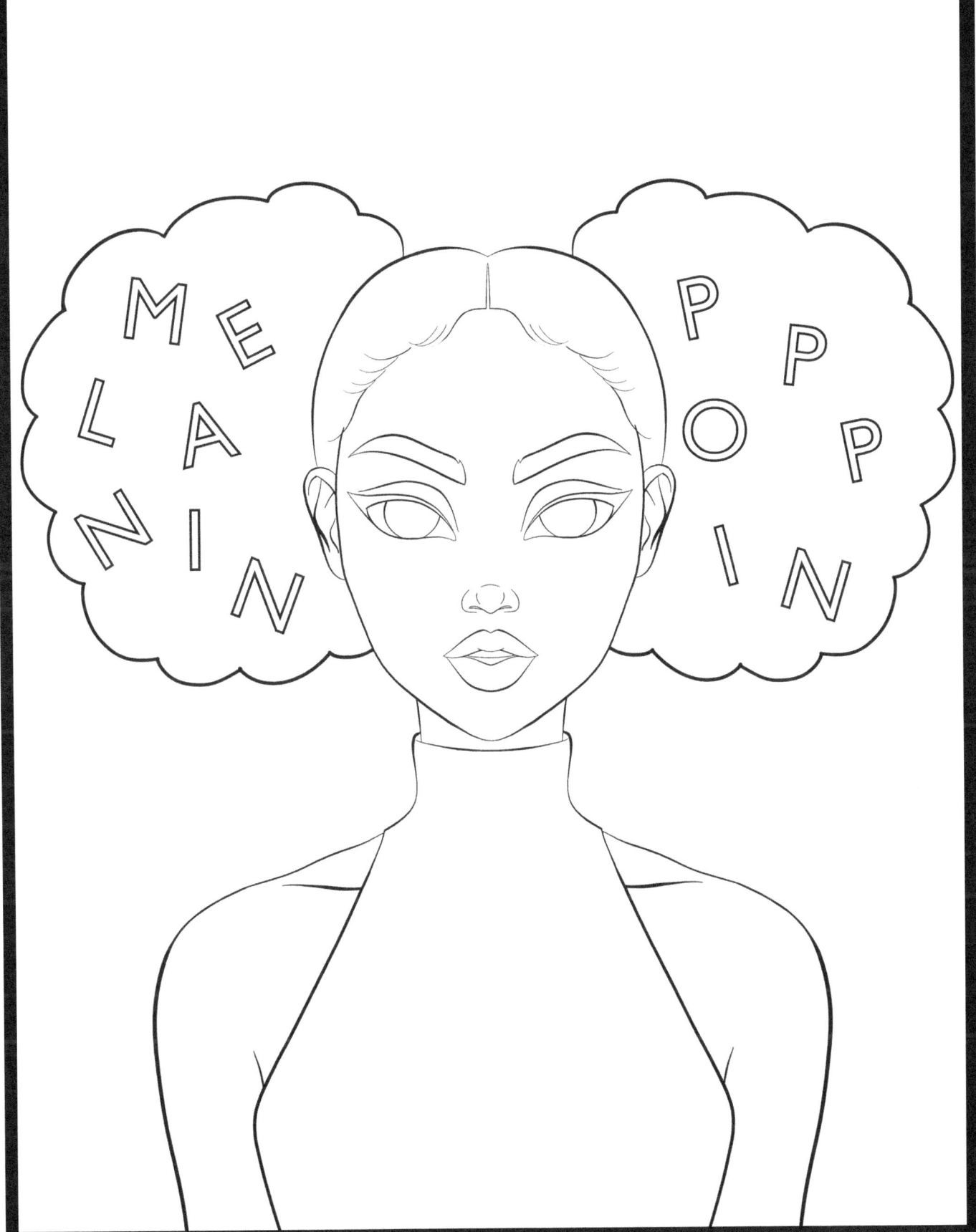

I AM WORTHY OF EVERYTHING GOOD IN LIFE.

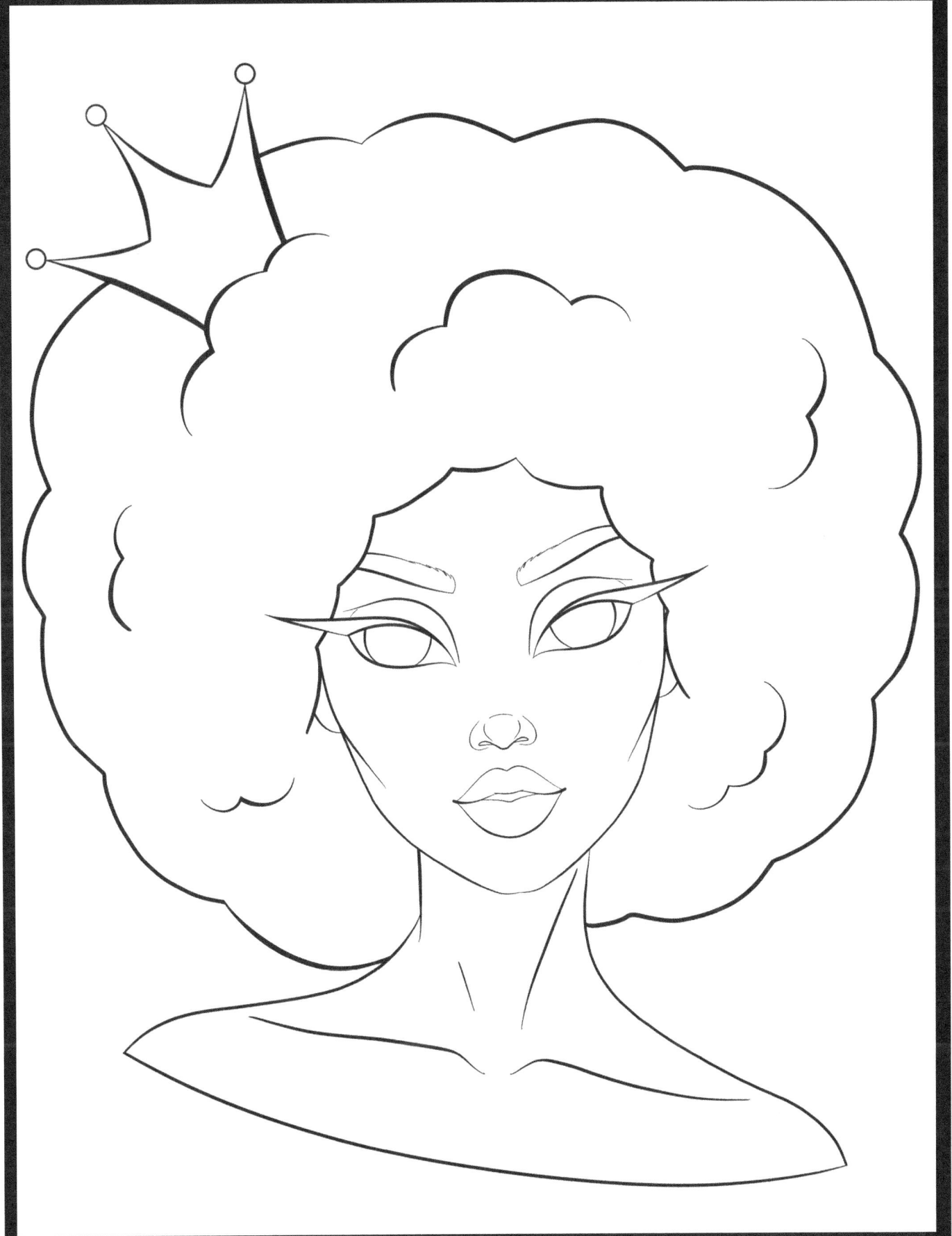

I AM WONDERFULLY MADE.

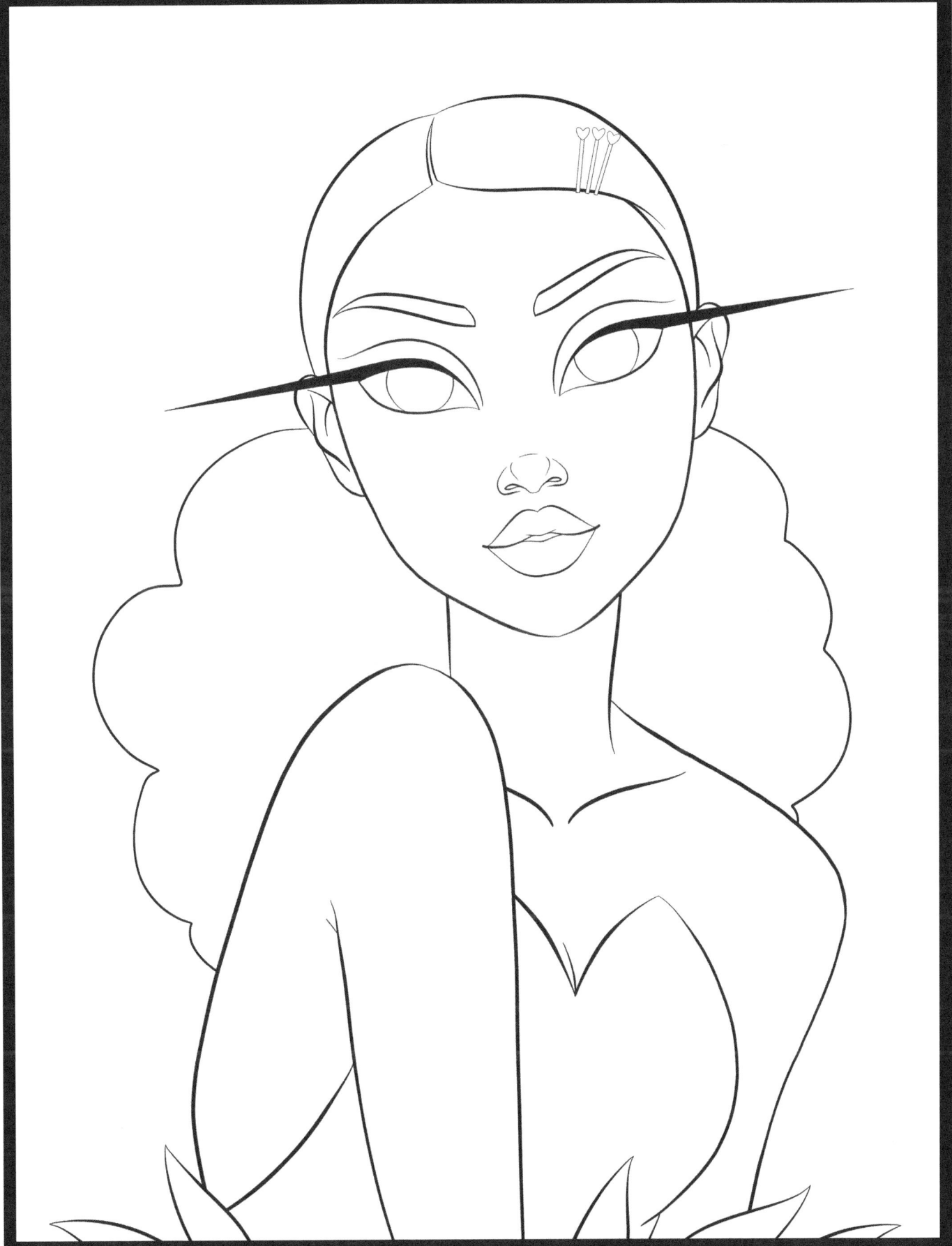

I EXUDE GOOD VIBES.

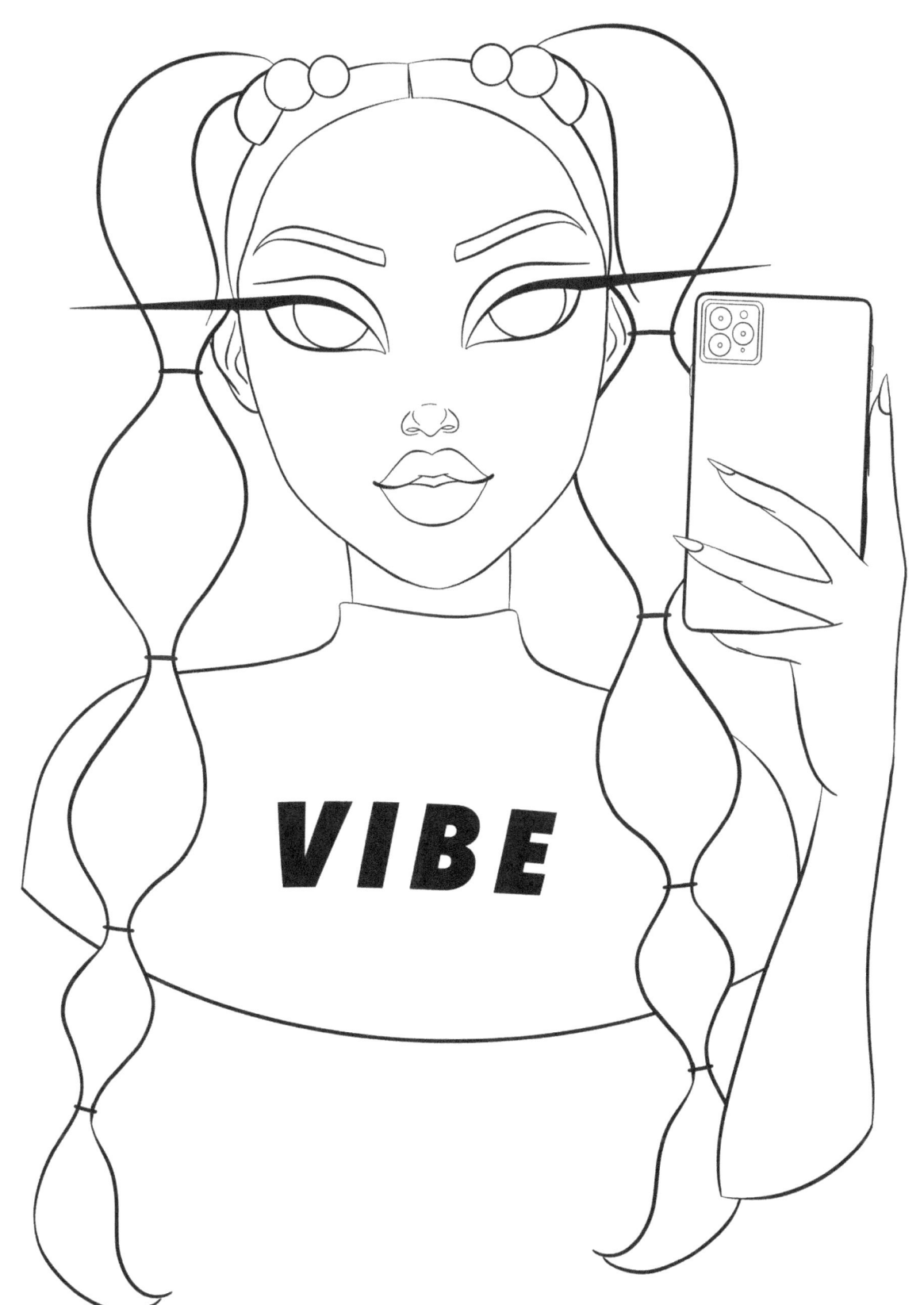

I RADIATE CONFIDENCE.

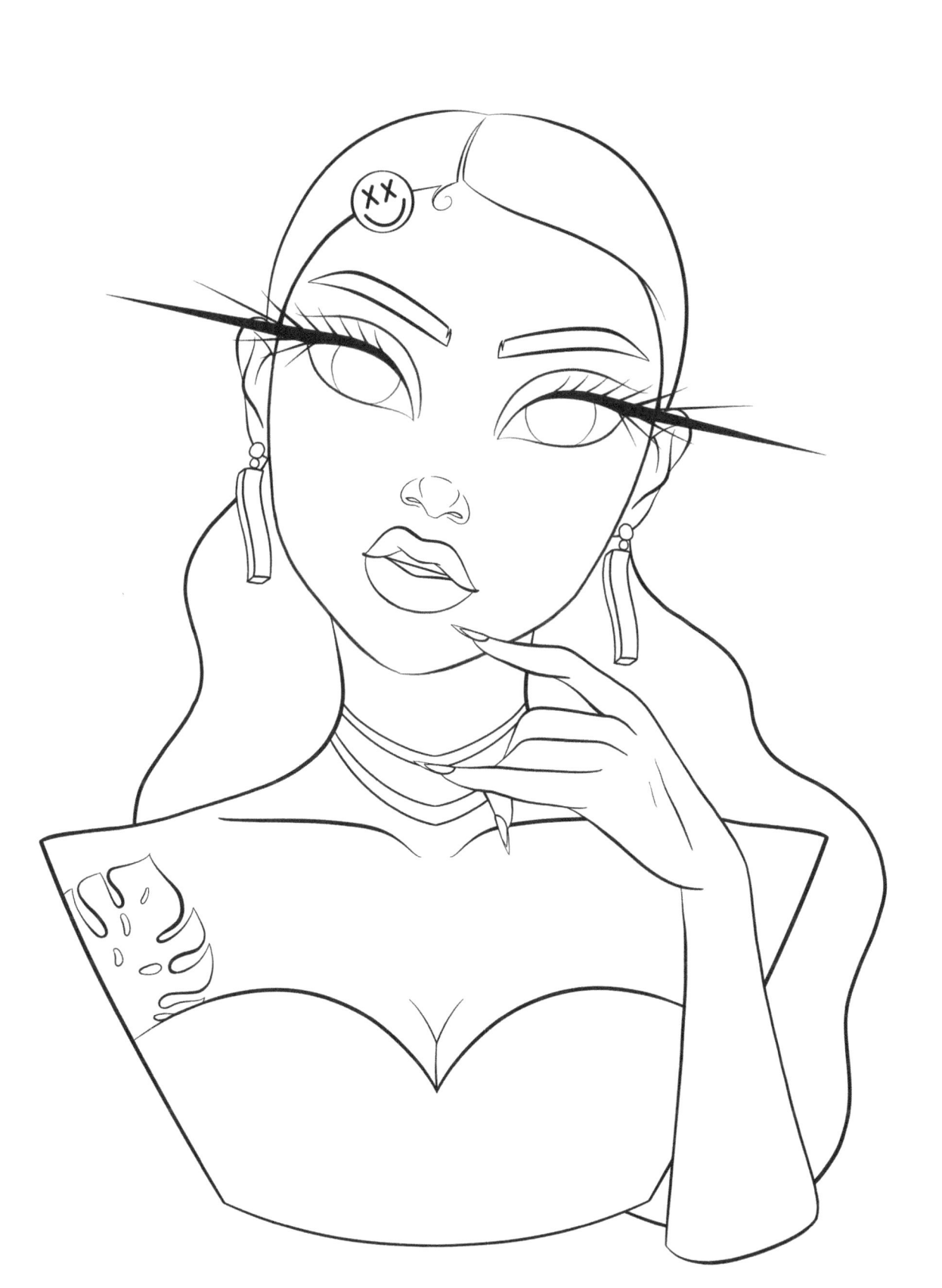

I AM A POWERHOUSE.

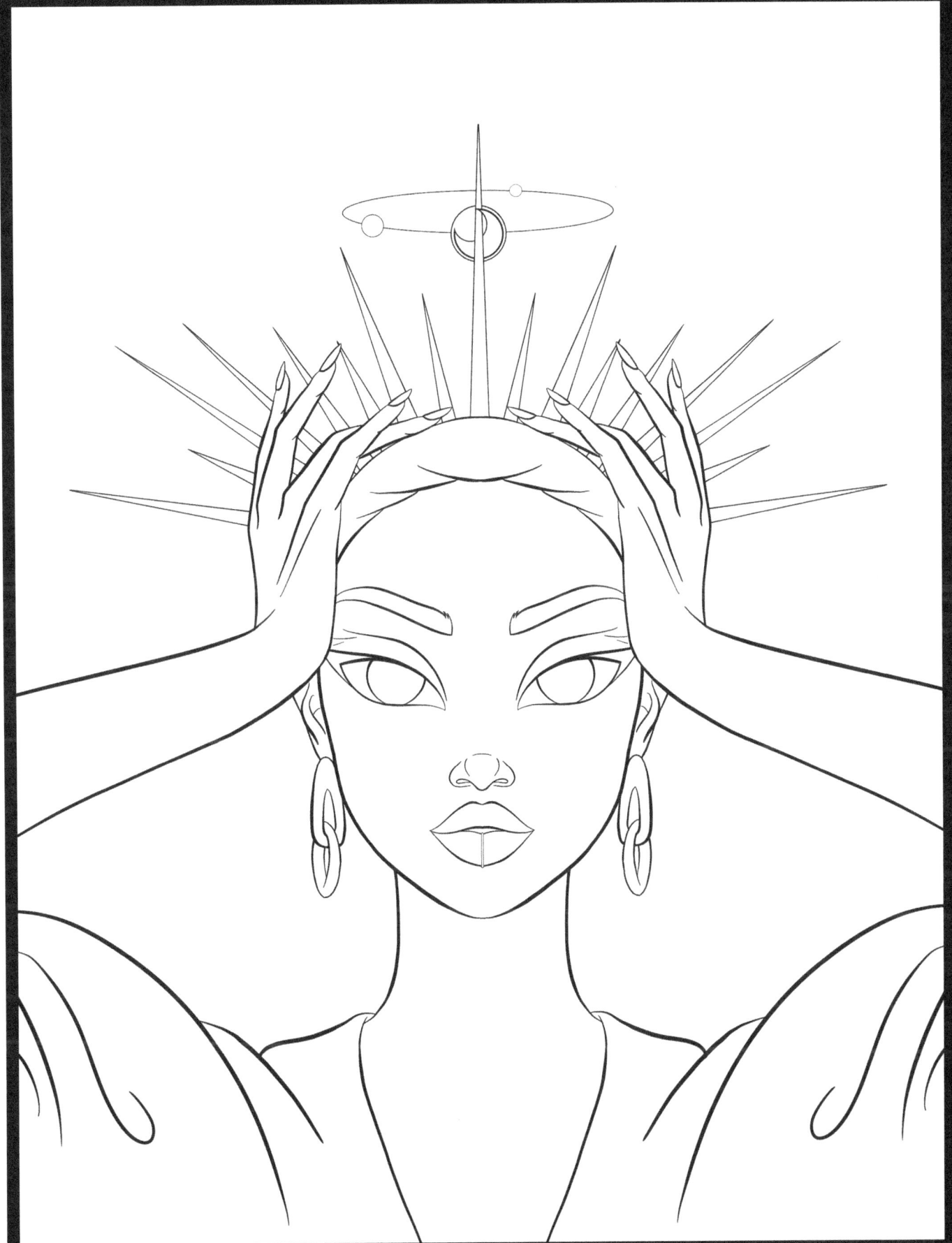

I AM ONE-OF-A-KIND.

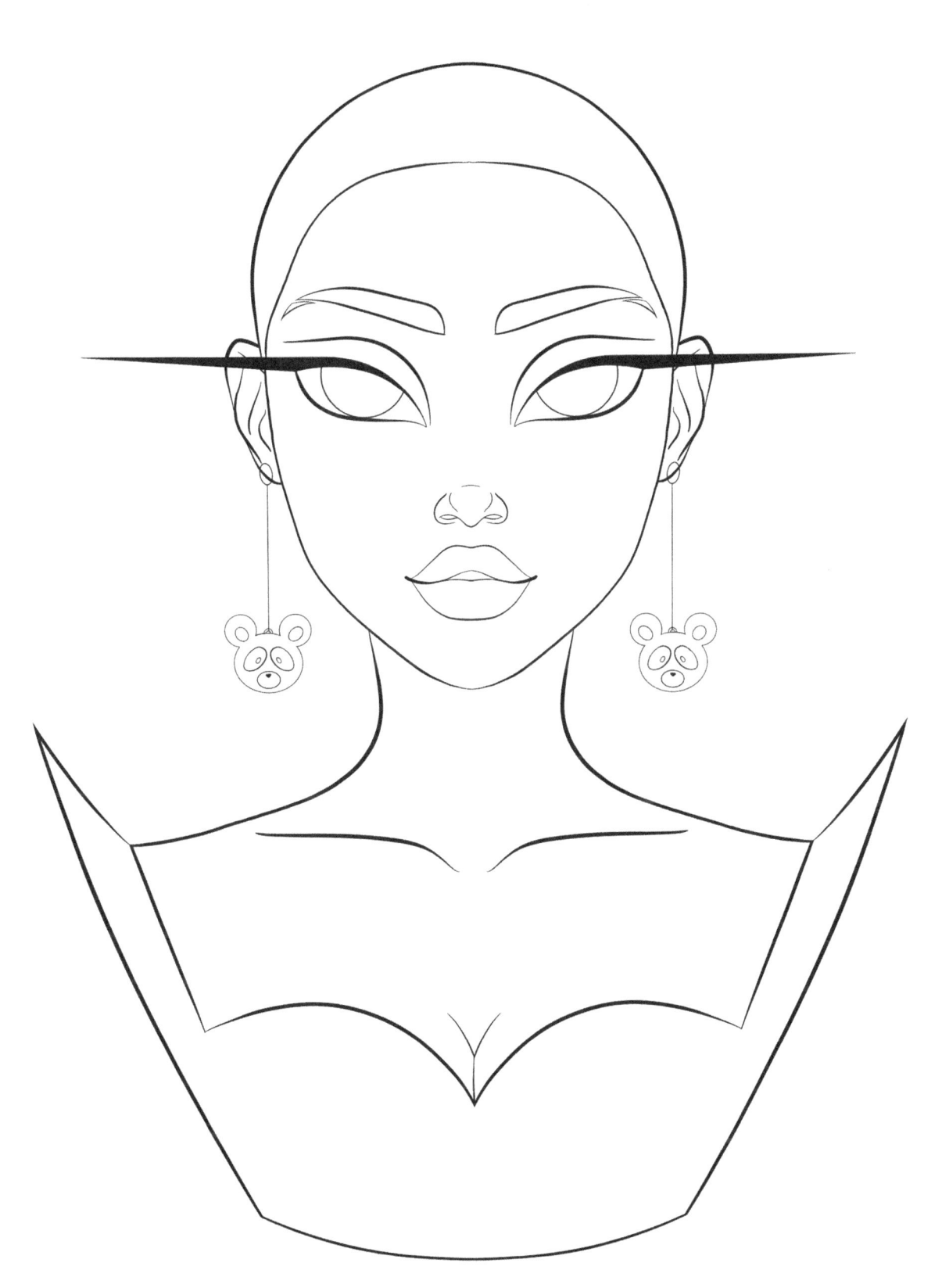

I AM DESTINED FOR GREATNESS.

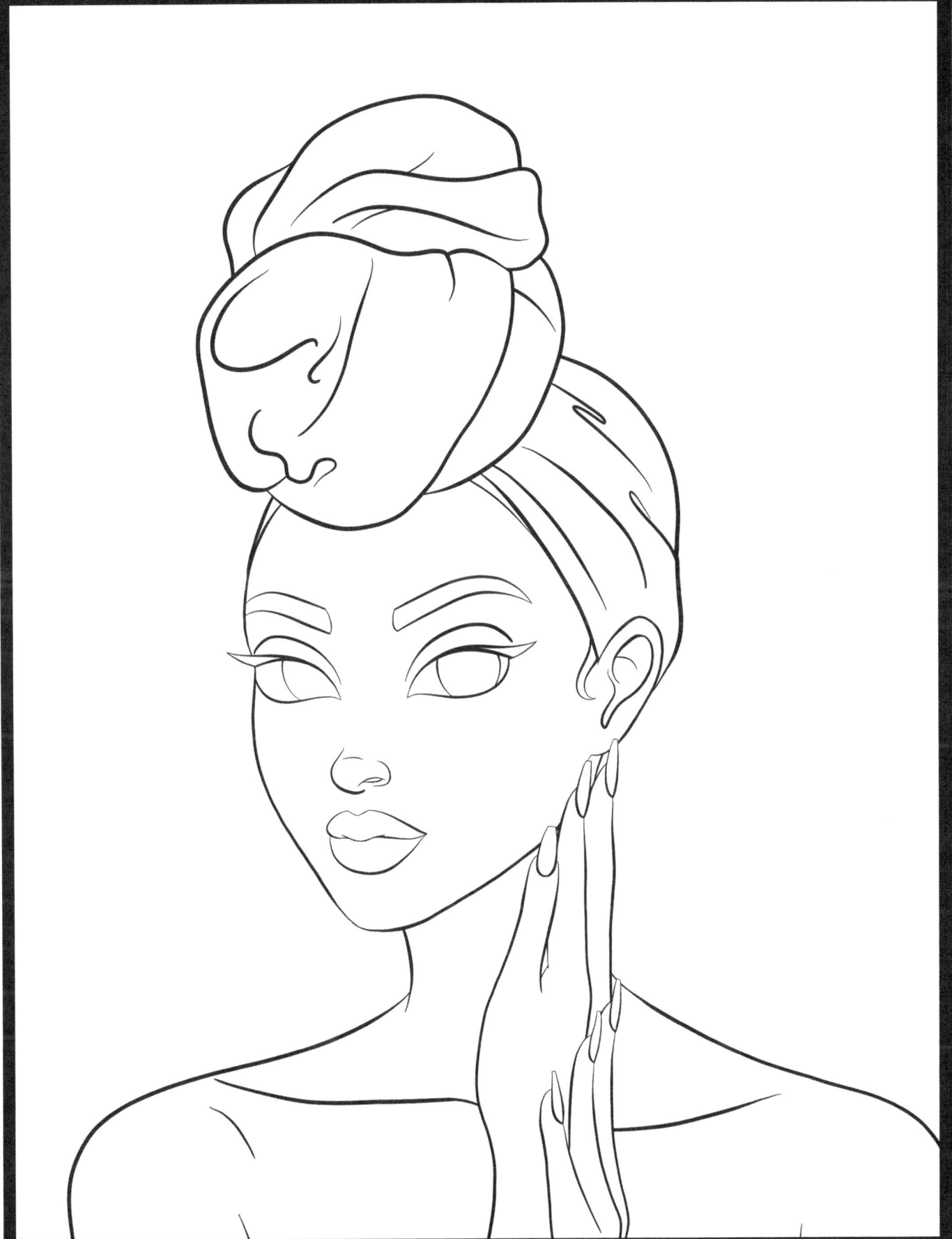

I RADIATE HAPPINESS AND LOVE.

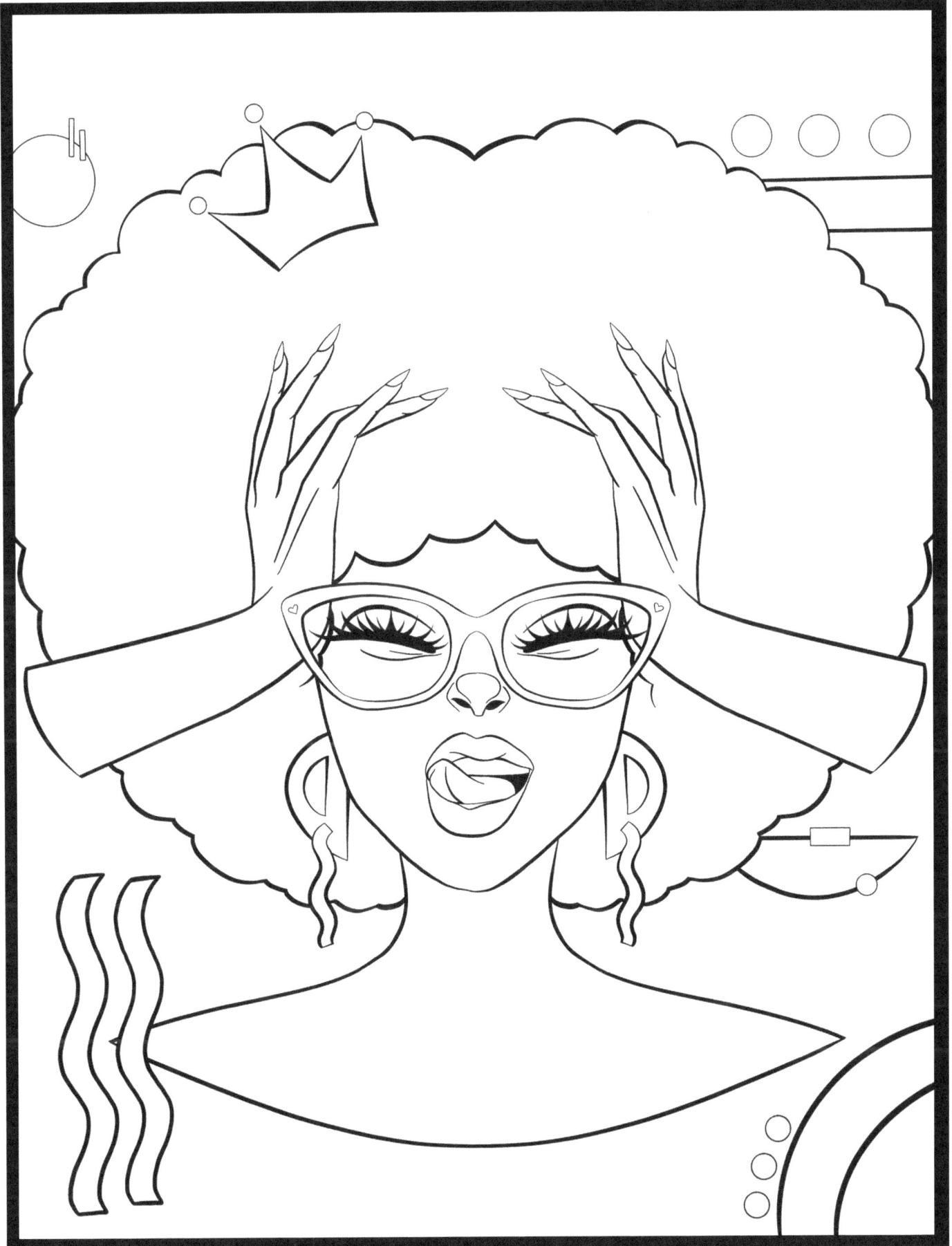

I AM ME,
& THAT'S MORE THAN ENOUGH.

www.ingramcontent.com/pod-product-compliance
Lightning Source LLC
Chambersburg PA
CBHW081103240526
45465CB00026B/3306